ALFRED'S BASIC GUITAR THEORY 1 & 2

Contents

Alfred Music
P.O. Box 10003
Van Nuys, CA 91410-0003
alfred.com

ISBN-10: 0-7390-4896-1
ISBN-13: 978-0-7390-4896-2

Guitar photo courtesy of Taylor Guitars

Alfred Cares. Contents printed on
environmentally responsible paper.

How Sounds are Produced on the Guitar

The sensation of sound is caused by sound waves striking the eardrum. Then the waves are transmitted to the brain. Three things must be present if a sound is to be heard:

1. **The generator**. This causes the sound waves to be formed. A sound wave consists of thicker and thinner vibrations of molecules. The generator can be the vocal cords (as in the human voice), a reed (as on a clarinet or saxophone), the player's lips (as on a trumpet or trombone), a stretched skin (as on a drum), or a string (as on a violin, piano or guitar).

2. **The transmitting medium**. In order for the sound wave to reach the ear it must travel through air, water, or even a solid object like a wall. Sounds cannot travel in a vacuum; the most violent explosion in the vacuum of outer space will not be heard at all because there is no transmitting medium.

3. **The receiver**. In human beings and animals, this is the eardrum, a tightly stretched membrane inside the ear. When sound waves strike the eardrum, they cause it to vibrate. This vibration is converted to electrical impulses which stimulate the brain, and cause the sensation of sound. When a guitar string is plucked, it starts to vibrate. This vibration causes waves in the air. When these waves strike the eardrum, they cause it to vibrate at the same rate as the guitar string.

A string vibrates . . .   *. . . creating a sound wave . . .*   *. . . that strikes the eardrum . . .*   *. . . and is transmitted to the brain.*

Pitch

Pitch is the word musicians use when they want to refer to how high or low a sound is. Pitch is caused by vibration. Faster vibration causes higher pitch. Slower vibration causes lower pitch. For example, a note that vibrates at 440 vibrations per second (vps) is perceived by the ear to be higher than a note that vibrates at 220 vps, and lower than a note that vibrates at 880 vps. Most people can hear low notes that vibrate as slowly as 20 vps. High notes can be heard up to 15,000 or even 20,000 vps. Certain animals, especially dogs, can hear much higher than even these notes. The lowest open string on a guitar vibrates at 82.5 vps, the highest at 330 vps.

On the guitar there are three ways to change the pitch of a string:

1. Turning the tuning or machine head causes the string to become tighter or looser. Tighter makes the pitch rise. Looser makes the pitch drop.

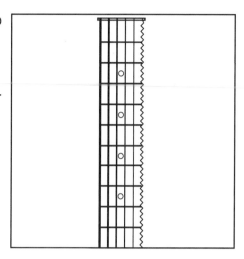

◀ *String vibrates for its full length. Make note of the pitch.*

2. Placing a finger of the left hand on any fret of a string effectively shortens the length of that string. As the finger slides closer to the bridge, the string length gets shorter and the pitch rises. Shorter makes the pitch rise. Longer makes the pitch drop.

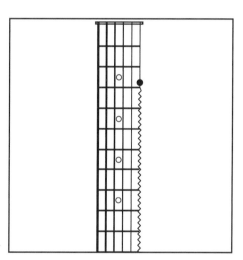

▲ *Finger on 3rd fret. String is shortened and the pitch rises.*

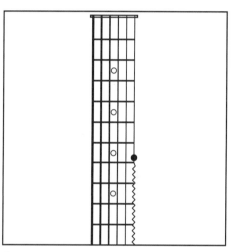

▲ *Finger on 7th fret. String is shortened even more and the pitch rises further.*

3. Pushing or bending a string across the fingerboard increases the string's tension even more and causes the pitch to rise. This bending effect is often used by blues and rock players.

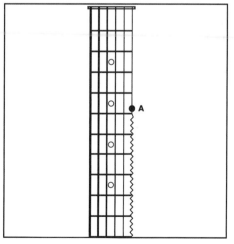

▲ *Finger on 5th fret. The note A vibrates at 440 vps.*

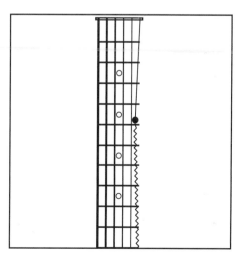

▲ *String is pushed or bent across fingerboard. Tension is increased and pitch rises.*

Notes

Notes are the basic units of music. Written music uses various shapes to indicate the different types of notes:

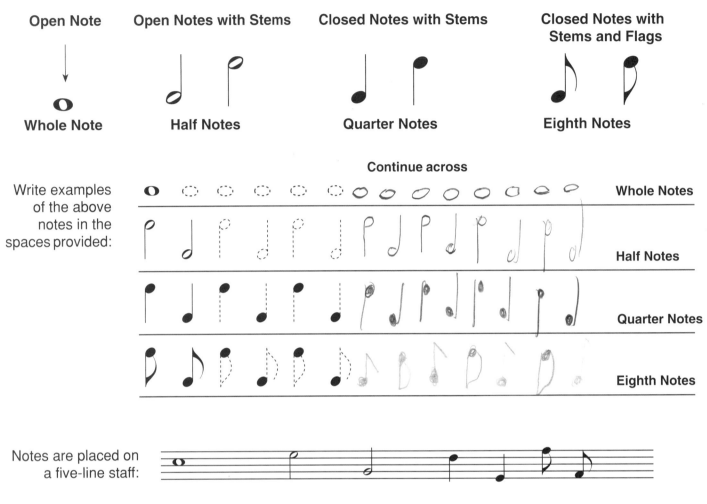

Open Note	Open Notes with Stems	Closed Notes with Stems	Closed Notes with Stems and Flags

Whole Note · **Half Notes** · **Quarter Notes** · **Eighth Notes**

Write examples of the above notes in the spaces provided:

Continue across

Whole Notes · Half Notes · Quarter Notes · Eighth Notes

Notes are placed on a five-line staff:

Music for the guitar is written in the **treble clef**.
The treble clef sign is placed before each five-line staff. The treble clef sign looks like this:

It is derived from the Gothic letter G:

Here's how to make it: First, draw kind of a long skinny J. Then add the rest of the sign; make sure the tail curls around the second line of the staff.

Continue across

Bar lines are vertical lines that divide the staff into **measures**. The measures show the basic pulse of the music and make reading music easier by dividing the notes into shorter groups.

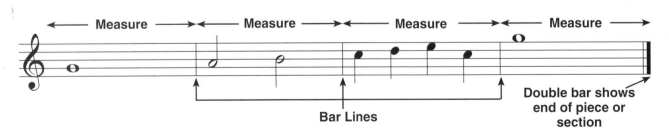

Measure — Measure — Measure — Measure

Bar Lines

Double bar shows end of piece or section

*This Theory book is correlated page-for-page with Alfred's Basic Guitar Method, books 1 and 2.

24.5/25

Naming the Notes

In music, notes are named by using the letters A, B, C, D, E, F and G. No other letters are used. Notes are placed on the five-line staff, either in the spaces or on the lines.

Notes in the spaces

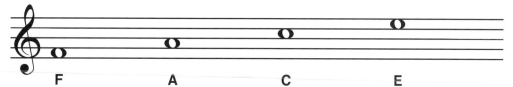

F   A   C   E

Notes on the lines

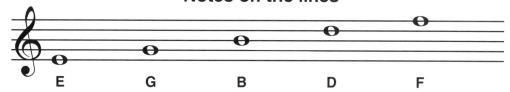

E   G   B   D   F

You can use these memory tricks to help you identify the notes:

Notes in the spaces (from low to high) spell the word **F A C E.**

Notes on the lines: **E**very **G**ood **B**oy **D**oes **F**ine.

Identify the following notes and write their names in the spaces provided below each staff.

Notes in the spaces:

F   A   C   E   C   F   A   E   A   C   E

Notes on the lines:

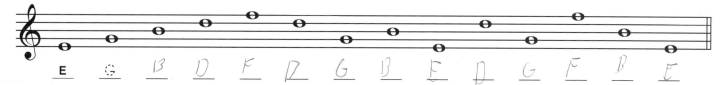

E   G   B   D   F   D   G   B   E   D   G   F   B   E

Mixed examples:

E   A   G   D   C   E   F   B   E   C   D   F   C   F   B

Below the staff are note names; write the actual notes on the staff:

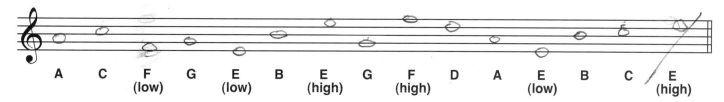

A   C   F   G   E   B   E   G   F   D   A   E   B   C   E
        (low)   (low)   (high)   (high)   (low)   (high)

Use after page 8 of
Alfred's Basic Guitar Method, Book 1.

Notes on the First String, the E String

21/23

Introducing . . .

E   F   G

The notes E, F and G are played of the 1st string.
Write their names in the spaces provided below the staff:

E   F   G   E   F

G   E   E   F   G   E

E   F   G   G   F   E   E   E   E   G   F   E

Using whole notes, write the notes on the staff that are called for below:

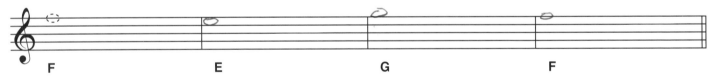

F   E   G   F

Do a similar exercise using half notes:

E   F   G   E   F   G   E   E

Do a similar exercise using quarter notes:

G   F   G   F   F   E   F   E   G   E   G   E   F   E   F   G

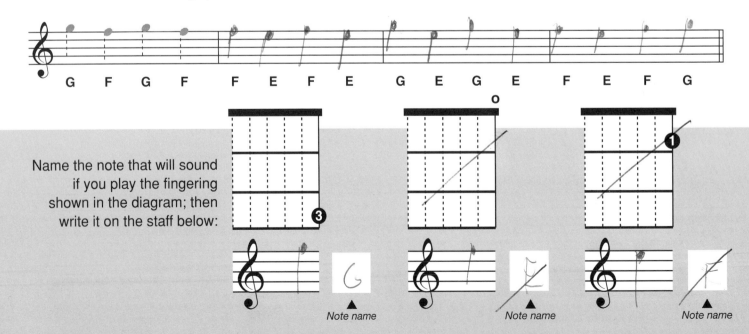

Name the note that will sound
if you play the fingering
shown in the diagram; then
write it on the staff below:

G
▲
Note name

F
▲
Note name

F
▲
Note name

Rhythm:
Quarter, Half, Dotted Half and Whole Notes

As you have already seen, the pitch of a note (how high or low) is indicated by its position on the five-line staff. The duration of a note (how long it sounds) is indicated by its shape.

Imagine a steady beat like a clock ticking. Tap your foot to this beat.

Now play any open string on the guitar, once for each beat. These notes are called **quarter notes** and they are written like this:

Half notes get two beats and are written like this:

Dotted half notes get three beats and look like this:

Whole notes get four beats and look like this:

Write the number of beats each of the following notes gets:

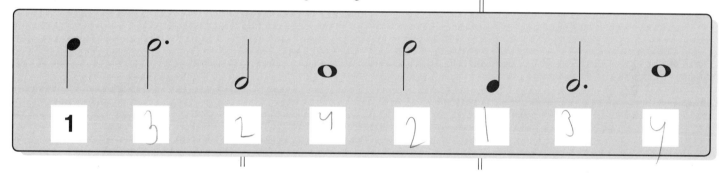

Time Signatures

Each piece of music starts with a clef, immediately followed by a **time signature**. The upper number tells you how many beats there are in each measure, the bottom number tells you what kind of note gets one beat (4=quarter note).

A time signature of **4/4** tells you there are four beats in each measure and a quarter note gets one beat.

A time signature of **3/4** tells you there are three beats in each measure and a quarter note gets one beat.

Practice writing these two time signatures on the staffs provided below:

Continue across

Continue across
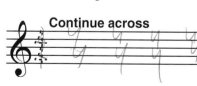

Use after page 12.

Notes on the Second String, the B String

B   C   D

The notes B, C and D are played on the 2nd string.
Write their names in the spaces provided below the staff:

B   C   D   C   B   D   C   B   B

C   B   C   D   B   D   B   C

Write a similar exercise using notes on the 1st and 2nd strings:

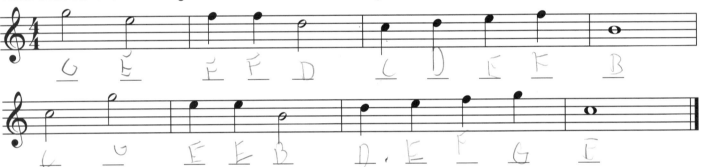

G   E   F   D   C   D   E   E   B

C   G   E   B   D   E   F   G   E

Using quarter notes, draw the notes on the staff that are called for below:

B   C   D   E   F   G   E   D   C   B   D   F   G   F   E   C

Do a similar exercise using dotted half notes: (If the note is in a space, the dot goes directly to the right of the note head. If the note is on a line, the dot goes a little above the line and to the right of the note head.)

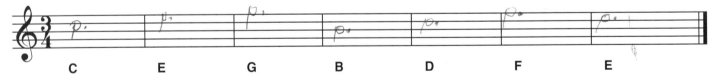

C   E   G   B   D   F   E

Do a similar exercise using half notes and whole notes:

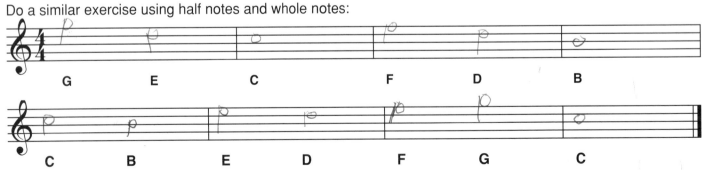

G   E   C   F   D   B

C   B   E   D   F   G   C

IMPORTANT: While it is not necessary to play the writing exercises in this theory book, the benefit to the student will be reinforced by performing appropriate sections.

More on $\frac{4}{4}$ and $\frac{3}{4}$ Time

24/25

As you have already learned, every measure of $\frac{4}{4}$ must contain four beats. Complete the following measures, making sure that each one contains four beats. Use the notes called for below the staffs. Point all note stems down. Add only one note per measure.

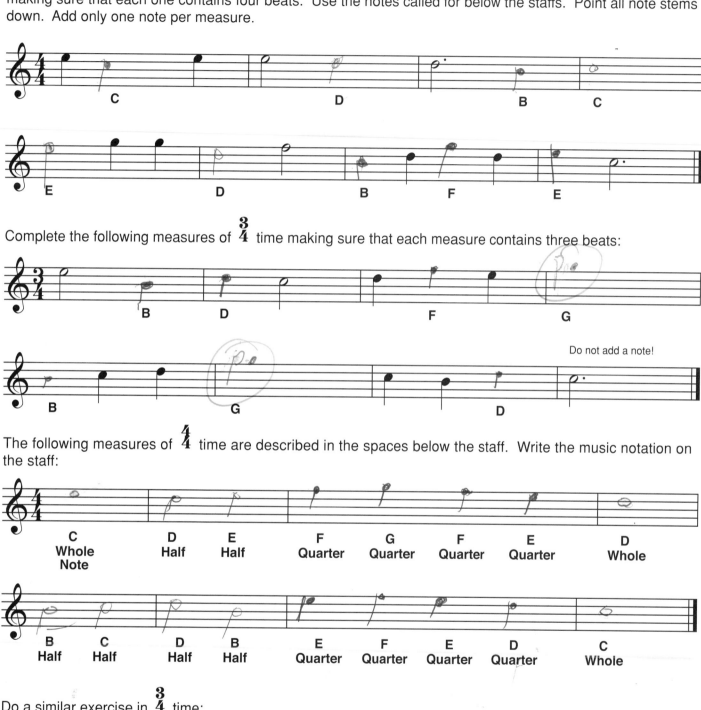

Complete the following measures of $\frac{3}{4}$ time making sure that each measure contains three beats:

Do not add a note!

The following measures of $\frac{4}{4}$ time are described in the spaces below the staff. Write the music notation on the staff:

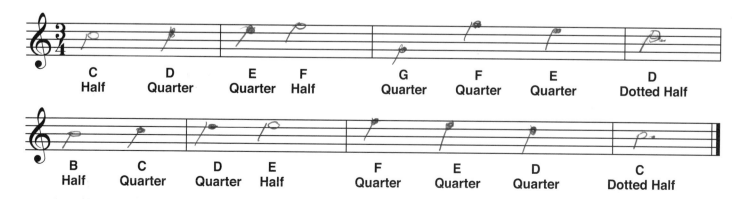

Do a similar exercise in $\frac{3}{4}$ time:

Stemming

19/20

Use after page 17.

When writing notes that have stems—quarters, half notes and dotted half notes—keep in mind two things:

1. Any note written on middle line B or higher gets a down stem. Any note lower than middle line B gets an up stem.

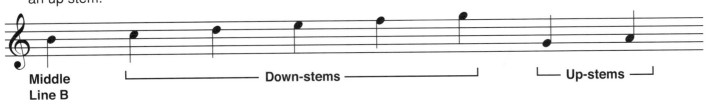

Middle Line B —— Down-stems —— —— Up-stems ——

2. To make your stems look more professional, make sure they go straight up and down, and that they are approximately as long as three spaces and a line, or three lines and half a space. See below. Then write your own examples.

3 spaces and a line   **3 lines and half a space**   **Add stems to these noteheads**

Introducing . . .
G   A

Notes on the Third String, the G string

The notes G and A are played on the 3rd string.
Write their names in the spaces provided:

G   A   A   G   A   A   G   A   G   G   A

Recognizing the Notes on the First Three Strings

Write the names of the notes in the spaces provided:

G   A   B   C   B   E   E   D   C   B   G

G   E   E   E   D   C   B   C   D   E   C

G   E   C   E   D   B   E   C   A   D

G   B   D   E   D   B   C   E

Recognizing the Three-String C Chord

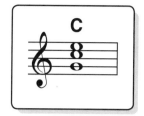

A chord is a combination of two or more harmonious notes.
The staff below contains various chords. Write a C in the space
provided above the chords that are the three-string C chord.
Leave the chords you do not recognize blank.

The following C chords are each missing one or more notes. Fill in the missing notes:

Arpeggios

An arpeggio (pronounced "ar-PED-jee-o") means that the notes of a chord are played one at a time rather than simultaneously. The word arpeggio is an Italian word that means "like a harp."

Some of the following arpeggios are based on a C chord. Others are not. Write a "C" above the ones you recognize. Arpeggios may be played from the lowest note to the highest, or from the highest note to the lowest.

Broken Chords

Sometimes a chord is broken into a combination of single notes and two-note chords. In the spaces above the following broken chords, write a C over the broken chords based on the three-string C chord. Like arpeggios, broken chords may be played from the bottom up or from the top down.

Use after page 21.

Recognizing the Three-String G⁷ Chord

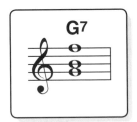

The staff below contains various chords. Write a G⁷ in the space provided above the chords that are three-string G⁷ chords. Then start over and write a C in the spaces above the three-string C chords.
Leave the chords you do not recognize blank.

The following G⁷ chords are each missing one or more notes. Fill in the missing notes:

Some of the following arpeggios are based on G⁷; some are based on C. Write the names above the staff:

Some of the broken chords below are based on G⁷; some are based on C. Write the names above the staff:

Write the name of the chord that goes with each chord diagram. Then write its notes on the staff below:

Chord name ▶ _____   Chord name ▶ _____

Recognizing the Three-String G Chord

The staff below contains various chords. In the spaces above the staff write only the name of the G chords. You may then go back and write the names of the C and G^7 chords you recognize. Leave the chords you do not recognize blank.

The following G chords are each missing one or more notes. Fill in the missing notes.

Some of the following arpeggios are based on G; others are based on C or G^7. Write in the names of the chords that you recognize above the staff. The notes may be in any order and still be a C, G^7 or G chord.

Some of the broken chords below are based on G; others on C or G^7. Write the names above the staff:

Write the name of the chord that goes with each chord diagram. Then write its notes on the staff below:

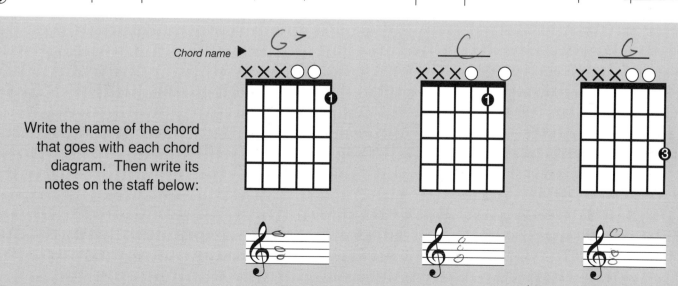

Use after page 22.

Reviewing the C, G⁷ and G Chords

The staffs below contain the C, G⁷ and G chords. Write their names in the spaces provided above the staffs:

Name the chord arpeggios notated on the staffs below. Notice the arpeggio variations.

Name the broken chords notated on the staffs below:

The following staffs combine chords, arpeggios, and broken chords. Name each chord in the spaces provided:

Use after page 24.

21/22

Notes on the Fourth String, the D String

D E F

These notes are played on the 4th string.
Write their names in the spaces provided:

D E F E F D E F D E D F

Recognizing the Notes on the First Four Strings

The following notes are played on the first 4 strings. Write their names in the spaces provided below the staffs:

D E E D E F D

A B C A B G A

D E E D E F D

G E F D G E

Octaves

The word octave (pronounced "OC-tiv") comes from the Latin word for eight (as in octet, octagon and octopus, which has eight arms). In music, an octave means two notes that are eight notes apart. This is important, because two notes an octave apart have the same letter name. The following examples show all the octaves you have learned so far. Write the names of the notes in the spaces provided:

D D E E F F G G

* HOLD SIGN (Fermata): This sign indicates that the time value of the note is lengthened (approximately twice its value).

Use after page 28.

Recognizing Four-String Chords (G & G⁷)

Introducing . . .

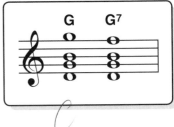

The staffs below contain four-string G and G⁷ chords, three-string C, G⁷ and G chords, and a few chords you won't recognize. Write the names of all the chords you do recognize in the spaces provided:

The following four-string G and G⁷ chords are missing one or more notes. Fill them in:

In the following example, broken chords and arpeggios are combined. Name the chords in the spaces provided:

18/18

Use after pages 30 and 31.

Notes on the Fifth String, the A String

Introducing . . .

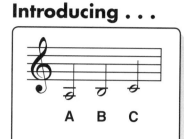

A   B   C

When notes are written above or below the five-line staff, extra short lines called **ledger lines** are added.

The following notes are found on the 5th string.
Write their names in the spaces below the staff:

A B C D A C B C A C B C B A

When adding ledger lines, make them about ¼ inch long and space them the same as normal staff lines.
Write the notes described on the staff below. All notes are played on the 5th string.

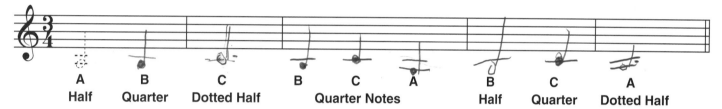

A	B	C	B	C	A	B	C	A
Half	Quarter	Dotted Half	Quarter Notes			Half	Quarter	Dotted Half

The following example uses all the octaves you have learned.
Write their names below the staff in the spaces provided:

A A B B C C D D E E

E F G G E E F F

D D C C A A B B C C

The following example uses notes from the first 5 strings of the guitar. Write their names in the spaces below:

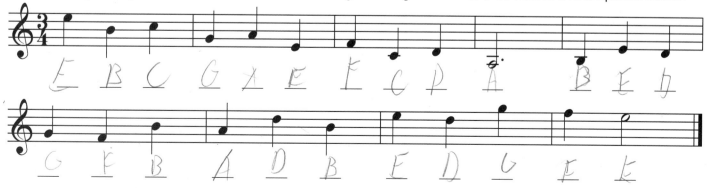

E B C G E E F C D A B E D

G F B A D B E D G E E

Use after page 35.

Incomplete Measures

Sometimes the 1st measure of a piece will contain *less* than the normal number of beats. This incomplete measure is called a pickup. Usually, if the 1st measure is a pickup bar, the last bar is also incomplete. When the beats of the 1st and last measure are added together, however, they will always equal one *full* measure.

Answer the following questions about pickups in $\frac{4}{4}$ time:

The 1st measure has a one-beat pickup; how many beats does the last measure have? __3__

The 1st measure has a three-beat pickup; how many beats does the last measure have? __1__

The 1st measure has a two-beat pickup; how many beats does the last measure have? __2__

These questions apply to $\frac{3}{4}$ time:

The 1st measure has a two-beat pickup; how many beats does the last measure have? __1__

The 1st measure has a one-beat pickup; how many beats does the last measure have? __2__

Below are some examples of pickups. In each case, complete the last measure with the proper number of beats, using only one note:

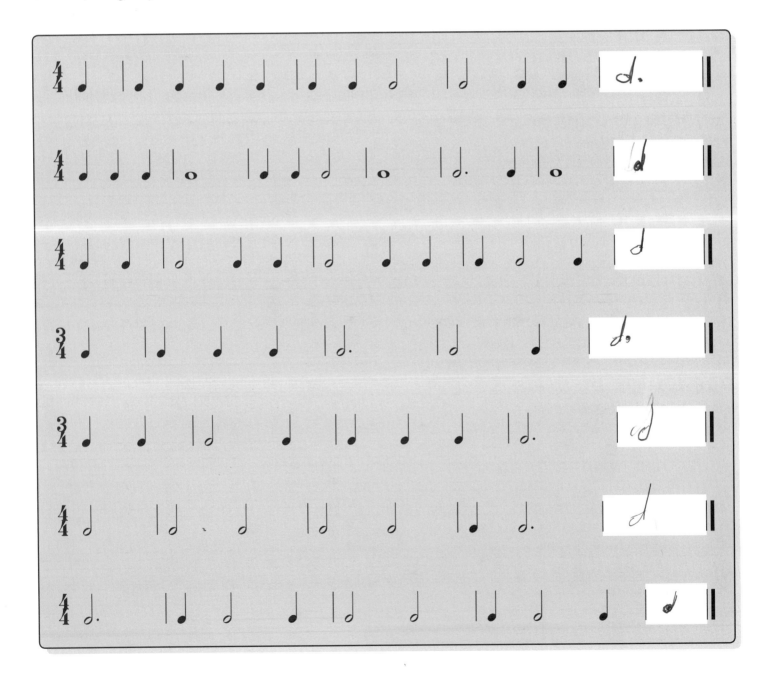

22/23

Notes on the Sixth String, the Low E String

Introducing . . .

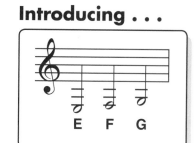

E   F   G

The following notes are found on the 6th string.
Write their names in the spaces provided:

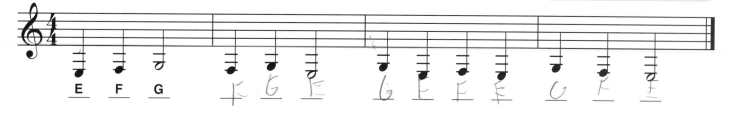

E   F   G   F   G   E   G   E   E   E   G   E

Write the notes described on the staff below. When writing stems on notes below B, extend the stems to the middle (3rd) line of the staff.

E	F	G	F	G	E	F	G	E
Half	Quarter	Dotted Half	Quarter Notes			Half	Quarter	Dotted Half

The following example uses the notes below the staff. First, see if you can name them rapidly. Then write their names in the spaces provided:

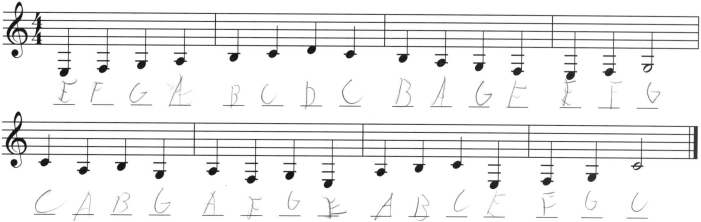

E F G A   B C D C   B A G E   E F G

C A B G   A E E   A B C E   F G C

The following example uses all the notes you have learned. See if you can name them rapidly. Then write their names in the spaces provided.

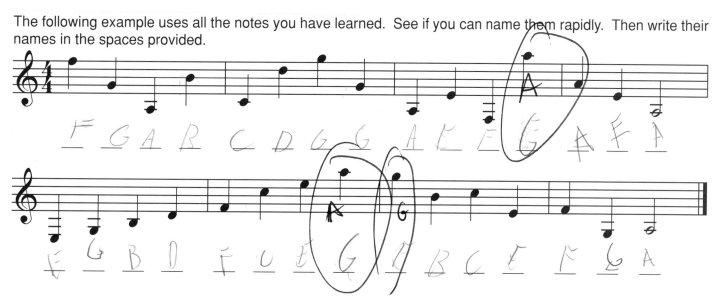

F G A R   C D G G   A E E G   A F A

E G B D   E E G   G B C E   E G A

✱ Complete

Use after page 40.

Rests

Rests in music are very important. They give the melody a chance to "breathe" and help the music achieve a graceful flow. Rests can also be very dramatic after a turbulent passage. The **quarter rest** 𝄽 has a value of one beat. In most cases it is centered on the staff between the 2nd and 4th lines. Practice writing a series of quarter rests on the staff below.

The **half rest** ▬ has a value of two beats. It is like a box that sits on the 3rd line of the staff. Practice writing it below:

The **whole rest** ▬ has a value of the number of beats in a complete measure. That is, in 4/4 it gets 4 beats; in 3/4 time the whole rest gets 3 beats. The whole rest is like a box that hangs from the 4th line of the staff. Practice writing it below:

In the following example some measures are missing beats. Complete them by inserting the appropriate rests. Important: the half rest is only used in 4/4 time; if a two-beat rest is required in 3/4 time, 2 quarter rests are used.

An easy way to remember the difference between half and whole rests is that the whole rest is heavier (longer) than the half rest, so that's why it hangs below the line. The half rest being lighter (shorter) floats on top of the line.

*Complete

Ties

A tie is a curved line that connects 2 or more notes of the same pitch. When 2 notes are tied, the 2nd one is not played separately. Rather, its value is added to the 1st note. For example, a half note (2 beats) tied to a quarter note (1 beat) is held for 3 beats. Here are some examples of tied notes. In the spaces provided, write how long each note is held separately, then write the total number of beats held.

Introducing Tied Notes

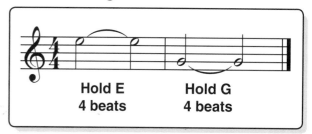

Hold E   Hold G
4 beats   4 beats

Example:

2   +   1 = 3 beats   7   +   3   =   7 beats

3   +   2 = 5 beats   1 + 1 = 2 beats

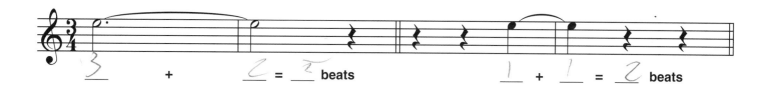

7   +   5   +   1 = 9 beats   1 + 3 = 4 beats

3   +   3   +   3   +   1 = 10 beats   2 + 2 = 4 beats

Drawing Ties

Connect the following notes with ties. Remember, when the stems go down, the ties curve up. When the stems go up, the ties curve down. Ties are always placed at the note heads.

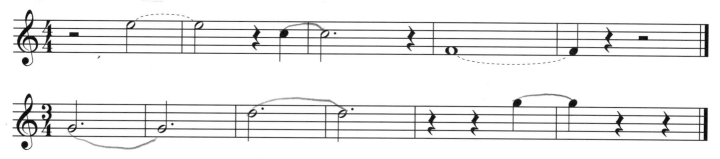

Eighth Notes

*stems
All Go Down Redo!

Use after page 46.

When 8th notes are written individually, they look like quarter notes with flags.

Practice writing 8th notes on the staff below:

etc.   etc.

In groups of 2 or more, 8th notes are written like quarter notes with a beam connecting the tops or the bottoms of the stems. Practice writing them below:

Eighth notes are played twice as fast as quarter notes. How many beats do two 8th notes get? __4__
Four 8th notes? __✓__ Six 8th notes? __24__ Eight 8th notes? __32__

Using only the note E in the examples below, fill in the missing beats with groups of 2, 4, 6 or 8 8th notes.
In $\frac{4}{4}$ time the beam never goes across the midpoint of the measure.

Correct: **Incorrect:**

Use only the note E.

Add 8th notes using the notes below the staffs:

G A D C   E F   E D   C D A G

Half Steps and Whole Steps

A **half step** is the smallest difference in pitch that can be written in our system of musical notation. On the guitar, a half step equals one fret. If a note is played on the 1st string-1st fret, a half step higher would be the 1st string-2nd fret; a half step lower would be the 1st string-open.

Make two dots on each of the following diagrams with the 1st dot showing where the written note is played and the 2nd dot (use a different color) showing where a note a half step *higher* is played:

Example:

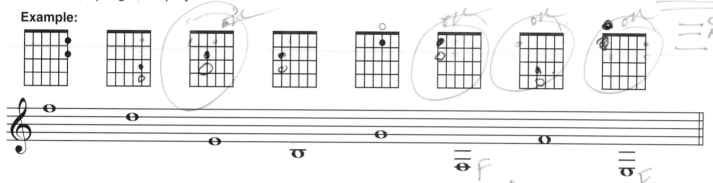

Do a similar exercise, but this time mark the place where a note a half step *lower* would be played:

Example:

A **whole step** equals two half steps. On the guitar, a whole step equals two frets. Do a similar exercise to those above, marking the place where the written note is found; then (in a different color) mark the place where a whole step *higher* is found:

Example:

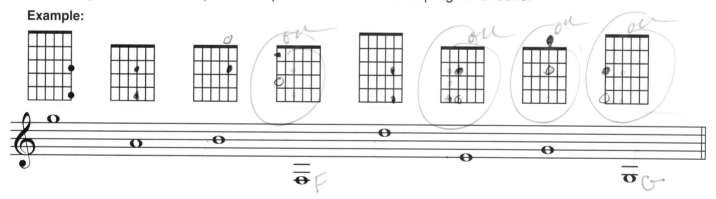

Continue similarly, marking where a note a whole step *below* the written note is found:

Example:

Use after page 50.

Sharps ♯ and Naturals ♮

The symbol ♯ is used to indicate a **sharp**. When placed in front of a note, it means to play that note a half step (one fret) *higher* than usual. The following examples have a natural note followed by the sharped note. Mark their positions on the diagrams above the staff. Use a different color for the sharped note.

A **natural** sign looks like this: ♮. When placed in front of a previously sharped note, it restores that note to its usual pitch. The following examples have a sharped note followed by the natural note. Mark their positions on the diagrams above the staff. Use black for the natural note and another color for the sharped note.

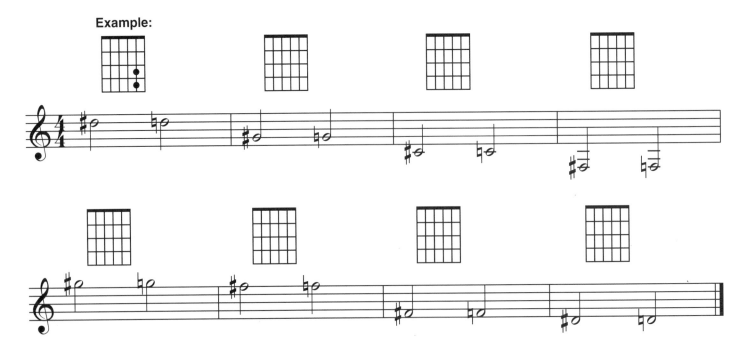

Use after page 50.

Flats ♭ and Naturals ♮

The symbol ♭ is used to indicate a **flat**. When placed in front of a note, it means to play that note a half step (one fret) *lower* than usual. The following examples have a natural note followed by the flatted note. Mark their positions on the diagrams below. Use a different color for the flatted note.

Example:

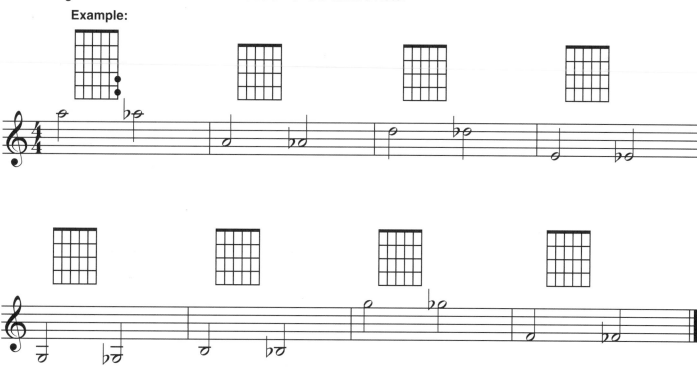

The same natural sign ♮ that is used for sharps is also used to restore flatted notes to their original pitch. The following examples have a flatted note followed by the natural note. Mark their positions on the diagrams above the staff, using a different color for the flatted notes:

Example:

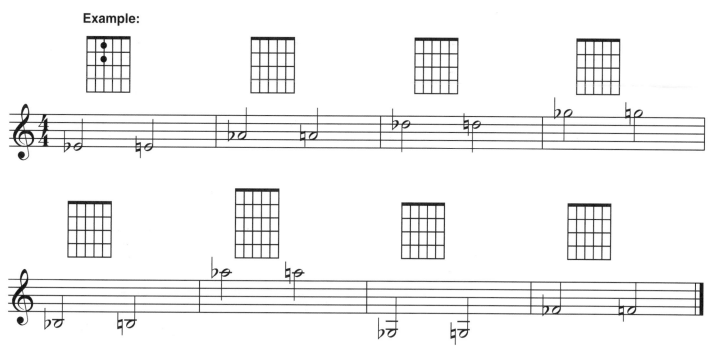

Use after page 51.

How to Flat Open Strings

Since an open string cannot be lowered further, another method must be found. Unlike the piano, the guitar is an instrument on which it is possible to find the same note in two or more places. This gives us a clue on flatting an open string. Let's take the high E string as an example. First, find this same E on *the 2nd string*. Since we know that D is played on the 2nd string-3rd fret, and since we also know that E is a whole step (two frets) above D, we can deduce that E can also be found on the 2nd string-5th fret. Try this on your guitar. If it is tuned properly, you'll hear that the 2nd string-5th fret sounds the same as the 1st string-open.

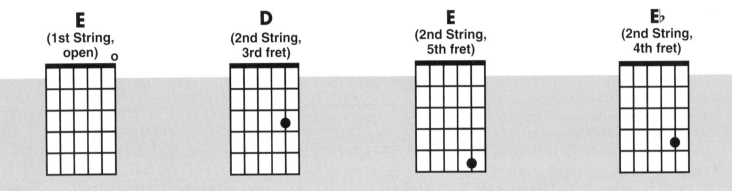

E
(1st String, open)

D
(2nd String, 3rd fret)

E
(2nd String, 5th fret)

E♭
(2nd String, 4th fret)

Once we know that E can be found on the 2nd string-5th fret, it is a simple matter to flat this note in the ordinary way. This means that E♭ is found on the 2nd string-4th fret. Using similar methods, figure out where to play the following flatted notes:

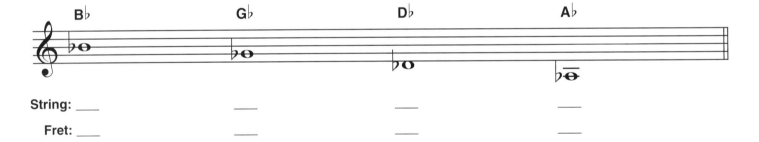

B♭   **G♭**   **D♭**   **A♭**

String: ___   ___   ___   ___

Fret: ___   ___   ___   ___

Enharmonics

Perhaps you've noticed that certain frets on the guitar can be named two different ways. For example, 1st string-2nd fret can be called either F♯ or G♭. 4th string-1st fret is either D♯ or E♭. These are called **enharmonic tones** or **enharmonics**. There are 5 commonly used enharmonic tones: C♯/D♭, D♯/E♭, F♯/G♭, G♯/A♭, and A♯/B♭. Less used but still important are E♯/F, B♯/C, F♭/E and C♭/B.

The Four-String D7 Chord

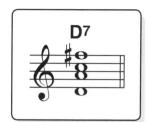

The staff below contains various four-string chords.

Write their names above the staff:

There are sharps missing in four different places in the following example. Write them in:

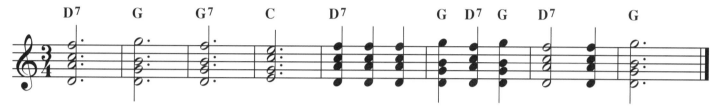

Write and label examples of the four-string C and G chords. Use half notes:

Write and label examples of the four-string G7 and D7 chords. Use quarter and half notes:

Write some quarter-note arpeggios (see page 11) of the four-string G7 and D7 chords:

Write some examples of broken chords using the four-string C and G chords:

Questions to Answer

The root of a chord is the note that names the chord.

What is the root of a G7 chord? ☐

What is the root of a C chord? ☐

What is the root of a D7 chord? ☐

What is the root of a G chord? ☐

Chords also contain other notes beside the root.

What notes does a C chord contain? ☐ ☐ ☐

What notes does a G chord contain? ☐ ☐

What notes does a G7 chord contain? ☐ ☐ ☐ ☐

What notes does a D7 chord contain? ☐ ☐ ☐ ☐

Major chords contain ☐ different notes.

Seventh chords contain ☐ different notes.

Use after page 56.

Building the C Major Scale

When building the C major scale
(or any major scale) use the following procedure:

1. Write down the keynote, the note that names the scale (C).

2. Add 7 more notes going up stepwise without skipping or repeating any letters (D E F G A B C).
    If you've done this correctly, the last note will have the same name as the keynote.

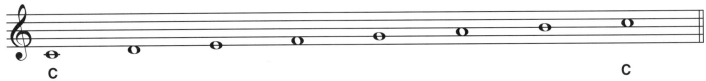

3. Write down the names of all the intervals in the scale (whole steps and half steps).

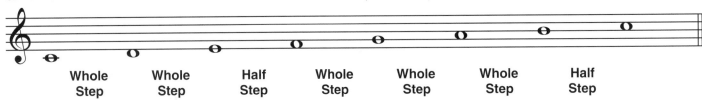

Whole Step	Whole Step	Half Step	Whole Step	Whole Step	Whole Step	Half Step

4. Check the intervals. They must occur in this order: whole, whole, half, whole, whole, whole, half.

Since the intervals in the C scale above do occur in the proper order, we now know that the notes of a **C major** scale are C D E F G A B and C. If the intervals did not occur in the proper order, we would still have a scale, but it would not be a major scale.

On the open staffs below, write the following:

An ascending C major scale in quarter notes—use proper stemming.

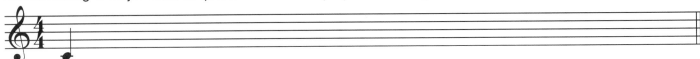

A descending C major scale in half notes—start with third space C:

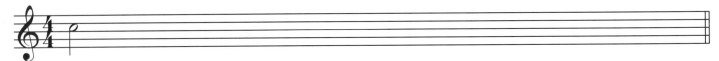

A C major scale in quarter notes that ascends from and descends back to low C:

Tetrachords

A **tetrachord** (*tetra* means four) is a group of 4 consecutive notes separated by 2 whole steps and a half step. C D E F is a tetrachord. G A B C is also a tetrachord. Major scales can be thought of as 2 tetrachords separated by a whole step.

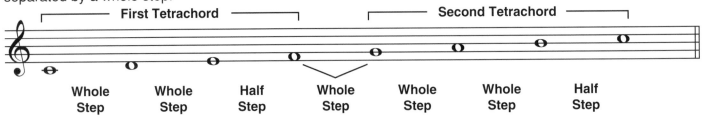

First Tetrachord			Second Tetrachord			
Whole Step	Whole Step	Half Step	Whole Step	Whole Step	Whole Step	Half Step

Use after page 56.

Building the G Major Scale

Use the same procedure as for the C major scale on the preceding page.

1. Write down the keynote (G).

2. Add 7 more notes going up stepwise without skipping or repeating any letters (A B C D E F G).

3. Write down the names of all the intervals in the scale (whole steps and half steps).

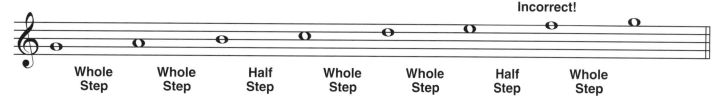

Incorrect!

| Whole Step | Whole Step | Half Step | Whole Step | Whole Step | Half Step | Whole Step |

4. Check the intervals. They must occur in this order: whole, whole, half, whole, whole, whole, half. Since they do not, some changes must be made.

Notice that the first 5 intervals (G to A, A to B, B to C, C to D, and D to E) do correspond to the major scale pattern. The next 2 intervals (E to F, and F to G) do not. E to F is only a half step; it should be a whole step. All you have to do is **sharp the F**. This makes the interval from E to F♯ a whole step, which is what it should be. It also means that the last interval in the scale is now F♯ to G, a half step, and this is now correct.

What this means is that to have a correct G major scale, you must sharp the F. Put another way, the correct G major scale consists of the notes G A B C D E **F♯** and G.

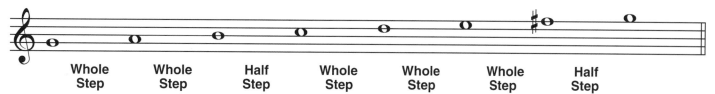

| Whole Step | Whole Step | Half Step | Whole Step | Whole Step | Whole Step | Half Step |

On the open staffs below, write the following: An ascending (one-octave) G major scale in quarter notes starting on low G.

A two-octave G major scale in half notes starting on low G and ending on high G.

A descending two-octave G major scale starting on high G and ending on low G. Use quarter notes.

IMPORTANT! Did you remember to sharp all the F's?

Use after page 56.

Building the F Major Scale

Use the same procedure as for the C major and the G major scales on the preceding pages.

1. Write down the keynote (F).

2. Add 7 more notes going up stepwise without skipping or repeating any letters (G A B C D E F).

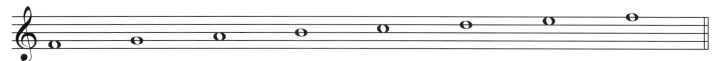

3. Write down the names of all the intervals in the scale (whole steps and half steps).

Incorrect!

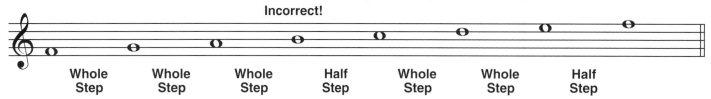

| Whole Step | Whole Step | Whole Step | Half Step | Whole Step | Whole Step | Half Step |

4. Check the intervals. They must occur in this order: whole, whole, half, whole, whole, whole, half. Since they do not, some changes must be made.

Notice that the first 2 intervals (F to G and G to A) are correct. The next interval (A to B) should be a half step, but it is a whole step. To fix this, **flat the B**. This makes the 3rd interval (A to B♭) a half step, and this is correct. Additionally, the next step in the scale (formerly B to C, an incorrect half step) is now B♭ to C, a whole step, which is correct. The rest of the scale corresponds to the whole whole half pattern and needs no further changes.

What this means is that to have a correct F major scale, you must flat the B. Put another way, the correct F major scale consists of the notes F G A **B♭** C D E F.

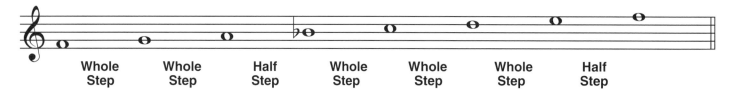

| Whole Step | Whole Step | Half Step | Whole Step | Whole Step | Whole Step | Half Step |

On the open staffs below, write the following:

A two-octave F major scale starting on low F. Use quarter notes.

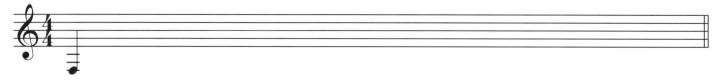

Write a two-octave descending F major scale in half notes. Start with top line F.

Important! Did you remember to flat all the B's?

Use after page 57.

Key Signatures

On the previous pages, you have learned that the key of C requires no sharps or flats; the key of G needs one sharp, and that sharp is F♯; the key of F requires one flat, and that flat is B♭.

Practice writing key and time signatures on the open staffs below. Here are some things to remember:

1. Every line begins with a clef.

2. Every staff also must begin with a key signature (unless it is in the key of C).

3. Only the first staff of a piece needs a time signature.

4. These three elements always go in the same order: clef, key signature, time signature.

Key of F in ¾ time

Key of G in ¾ time

Key of F in 4/4 time

Key of G in 4/4 time

Eighth Rests

Use after page 58.

Eighth rests mean to rest for the value of an 8th note, one half of a beat. In the following examples, add 8th rests in the appropriate places so that the measures are complete:

The Dotted Quarter Note

Dotted quarter notes receive one and a half beats; they are played the same as a quarter note tied to an 8th note. In the following measure, add 8th rests in the appropriate places so that the measures become complete. Then, using 1 & 2 & . . . write in the beats below the staff:

1 & 2 & 3 & 4 & continue

1 & 2 & 3 & continue

The First Position

Everything you've learned so far about the guitar lies in what is called the **first position**.
The first position includes the first 4 frets on each of the 6 strings. An exception, however,
is the high A on the 5th fret of the 1st string which is usually considered part of the first
position. The notes below can all be played in the first position. In the spaces below the
staffs, describe where to find the notes:

String: 1 ___ ___ ___ ___ ___ ___ ___ ___

Fret: 1 ___ ___ ___ ___ ___ ___ ___ ___

String: ___ ___ ___ ___ ___ ___ ___ ___ ___

Fret: ___ ___ ___ ___ ___ ___ ___ ___ ___

String: ___ ___ ___ ___ ___ ___ ___ ___ ___

Fret: ___ ___ ___ ___ ___ ___ ___ ___ ___

String: ___ ___ ___ ___ ___ ___ ___ ___ ___

Fret: ___ ___ ___ ___ ___ ___ ___ ___ ___

String: ___ ___ ___ ___ ___ ___ ___ ___ ___

Fret: ___ ___ ___ ___ ___ ___ ___ ___ ___

Did you remember your enharmonics? (E♯ = F, B♯ = C, F♭ = E, C♭ = B)

Reviewing Four-String Chords

The 4 chord diagrams below represent chords that you should know. Write their names in the spaces above the diagrams. Then write the actual notes that the chords consist of on the staffs below the diagrams:

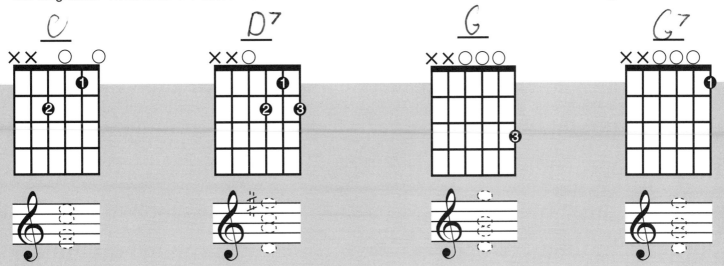

Using the chords above the staffs, write a rhythm guitar part in $\frac{4}{4}$ time. Use / / / / for repeated chords:

Using the 4 chords above, write an *arpeggio* accompaniment in $\frac{3}{4}$ time:

Using your own choice of chords, write a *broken chord* accompaniment in $\frac{4}{4}$ time. Add chord symbols first.

These Don't make sense

What's the rhythm?

Use after page 6.

Understanding Cut Time

The time signature **¢** stands for cut time. Also called by the Italian name "alla breve" ("A-luh BRAY-vuh"), it means that all note values get one half as many beats as they do in $\frac{4}{4}$ time. The rhythms will look the same as $\frac{4}{4}$ but the music goes by twice as fast. Cut time is used for marches (*The Stars and Stripes Forever*), fast show tunes (*If They Could See Me Now*), ragtime (*Bill Bailey*) and Dixieland jazz (*When the Saints Go Marching In*).

If you tap your foot when you play, you'll find it rather awkward when the tempo gets too fast. Since it's not unusual for tunes to be played at a tempo of M.M. ♩ = 240*, you'll find it much easier to tap your foot in cut time, at a tempo of M.M. ♩ = 120.

In the following examples, write the beats below the melody, first in $\frac{4}{4}$ time, then in cut time in the spaces provided.

Bill Bailey

The Stars and Stripes Forever

When the Saints Go Marching In

*M.M. = Metronome marking (beats per minute)

Use after page 7.

Understanding Repeat Signs

Double repeat signs look like this: ‖: :‖

The material between double repeat signs is played twice.

In the following example, the measures are played in this order: **1 2 3 4 1 2 3 4**.

If the repeat goes back to the beginning of the piece, the first double repeat sign is sometimes omitted. The next example is played exactly the same as the first example: 1 2 3 4 1 2 3 4.

First and second endings are used when only some of the measures are repeated.

1. Play from the beginning through the first ending (to the double repeat).

2. Play from the beginning a 2nd time. Skip the first ending and play the second ending instead.

In the example below, the measures are played 1 2 3 4 1 2 3 5.

D.C. al Fine stands for the Italian expression *Da Capo al Fine* ("dah CAH-po al FEE-nay) which means to go back to the beginning of the piece and play through to the word *"Fine,"* which is always at a double bar. The measures below are played 1 2 3 4 5 6 7 1 2 3 4.

D.S. al Fine stands for the Italian expression *Dal Segno al Fine* ("dal SENG-yo al FEE-nay"). It means go back to the sign that looks like 𝄋 and play the material through to the word *"Fine."*
The measures below are played 1 2 3 4 5 6 7 3 4.

36

D.C. al Coda means to go back to the beginning and play through to the coda sign that looks like ⊕. Then skip directly to the coda sign near the end of the piece. The 2nd coda sign also has the word Coda next to it. The measures below are played 1 2 3 4 5 6 1 2 3 7 8.

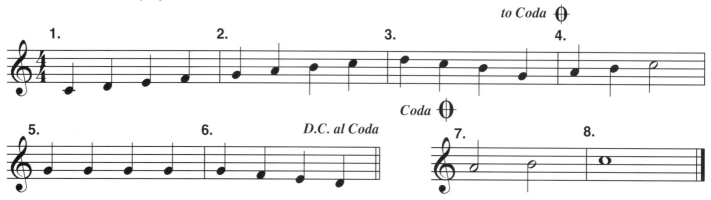

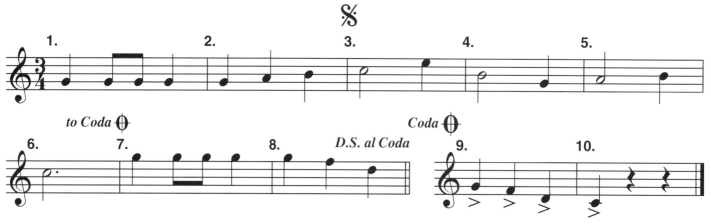

D.S. al Coda means to go back to the sign 𝄋 and play through to the coda sign ⊕. Then skip directly to the coda sign near the end of the piece. These measures are played 1 2 3 4 5 6 7 8 3 4 5 6 9 10.

> = Accent mark—play the note a little louder.

The sign 𝄎 means "repeat the previous measure." In the example below, the measures are played 1 1 3 3.

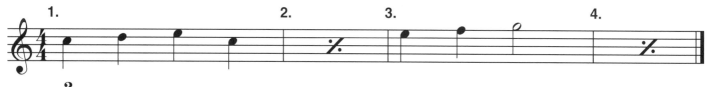

The sign 𝄎 means "repeat the previous two measures." In this example the measures are played 1 2 1 2 5 6 5 6.

The sign ╱ means "repeat the previous quarter note chord."

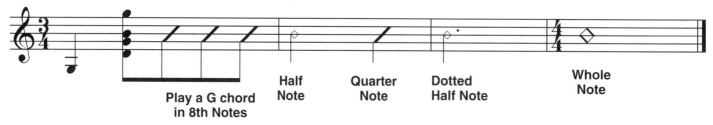

is played ⟶

The sign ╱ can be modified to show other rhythms.

Play a G chord in 8th Notes   Half Note   Quarter Note   Dotted Half Note   Whole Note

The Key of C Major

Use after page 8.

Pieces that are written in the key of C major:

1. have no key signature (no sharps or flats),

2. for the most part, make use of notes from the C major scale: C, D, E, F, G, A, B, C. Notes that are not in the C major scale are called **accidentals**. They are used occasionally, but the majority of the notes will come from the C major scale,

3. usually end on a C major chord.

The Three Principal Chords in the Key of C Major

The principal chords in a key are the three chords that are the most used. With them you can accompany thousands of folk, blues, country and rock songs such as *Oh, Susanna*, *Worried Man Blues*, *Wabash Cannonball*, *Blue Suede Shoes*, and even an occasional Christmas carol like *Silent Night*.

The three principal chords in any key are often referred to by using Roman numerals I, IV and V⁷. The easiest way to determine what the I, IV and V⁷ chords are in any key is to start with a two-octave major scale that belongs to the key. For example, to determine the three principal chords in the key of C, start with the two-octave C major scale:

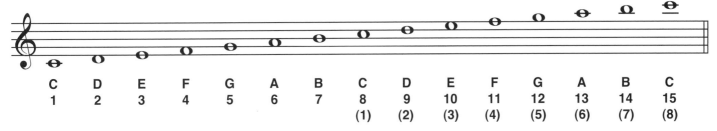

C	D	E	F	G	A	B	C	D	E	F	G	A	B	C
1	2	3	4	5	6	7	8	9	10	11	12	13	14	15
							(1)	(2)	(3)	(4)	(5)	(6)	(7)	(8)

The I, IV and V⁷ Chords in the Key of C Major

The I chord starts on the 1st scale tone, C. It contains 2 additional notes, which can be found by going up the scale and skipping a tone between each chord tone. Start with C (skip D), E (skip F), G. The I chord in the key of C major is a C major chord, which consists of the notes C E G.

The IV chord starts on the 4th scale tone, F. It contains 2 additional notes, which can be found by going up the scale and skipping a tone between each chord tone. Start with F (skip G), A (skip B), C. The IV chord in the key of C major is an F major chord, which consists of the notes F A C.

The V⁷ chord starts on the 5th scale tone. It contains 3 additional notes which can be found using the same method as before: G (skip A), B (skip C), D (skip E), F. The V⁷ chord in the key of C major is a G⁷ chord which consists of the notes G B D F.

Notes in a chord can appear in any order, and any note can appear more than once.

Questions to Answer

What are the three principal chords in the key of C?

Name the notes in an F major chord.

Name the notes in a G⁷ chord.

Name the notes in a C major chord.

Does the key signature of C major have any sharps?   Any flats?

The notes in the key of C major belong to what scale?

What chord does a piece in the key of C usually end on?

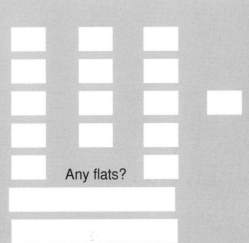

Use after page 8.

The Key of G Major

Pieces that are written in the key of G major:

1. have a key signature of 1 sharp. That sharp is F and means that all F's are played as F♯, unless preceded by a natural,

2. for the most part, make use of notes from the G major scale: G, A, B, C, D, E, F♯, G,

3. usually end on a G major chord.

The I, IV and V⁷ Chords in the Key of G Major

Start with the two-octave G major scale.

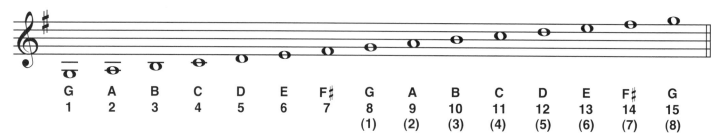

The I chord starts on the 1st scale tone, G. It contains 2 additional notes, which can be found by going up the scale and skipping a tone between each chord tone. Start with G (skip A), B (skip C), D. The I chord in the key of G major is a G major chord, which consists of the notes G B D.

The IV chord starts on the 4th scale tone, C. It contains 2 additional notes, which can be found by going up the scale and skipping a tone between each chord tone. Start with C (skip D), E (skip F♯), G. The IV chord in the key of G major is a C major chord, which consists of the notes C E G.

The V⁷ chord starts on the 5th scale tone, D. It contains 3 additional notes, which can be found by using the same method as before. Start with D (skip E), F♯ (skip G), A (skip B), C. The V⁷ chord in the key of G major is a D⁷ chord, which consists of the notes D F♯ A C.

Questions to Answer

What are the three principal chords in the key of G major?

Name the notes in a D⁷ chord.

What are the notes in a C major chord?

What are the notes in a G major chord?

What is the key signature of G major?

Which note is usually sharped in G major?

What chord does a piece in the key of G major usually end on?

Alternate Fingerings

As you learned when flatting open strings (page 26), there is more than one place on the guitar where a note can be found. This makes it possible to flat the open strings, and is also useful when choosing a fingering for certain passages. For example, the following figure is awkward to play when the open E string is used. When the same passage is played using E on the 2nd string-5th fret, the figure is not only easier to play, but also sounds smoother as it is now played on one string.

When figuring out alternate fingerings, it is useful to remember that every step in the C scale (C D E F G A B C) is a whole step, except for E to F and B to C, which are half steps. From this you can see that if D is played on the 2nd string-3rd fret, E must be a whole step or 2 frets higher, on the 2nd string-5th fret. Find the alternate fingerings of the following notes and write down the fret number where they are located.
Use a "o" for open strings.

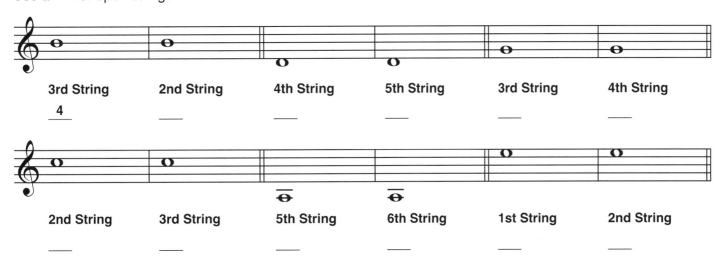

3rd String	2nd String	4th String	5th String	3rd String	4th String
4	___	___	___	___	___

2nd String	3rd String	5th String	6th String	1st String	2nd String
___	___	___	___	___	___

Alternate fingerings also allow us to play 2 notes together when the lower note seems to be on the same string. For example, when playing D and B together (see chart to the right) D is played on the 2nd string-3rd fret. Ordinarily B is also played on the 2nd string. Since it is impossible to play both notes on the same string, the B must be found on the next lower string. We already know that the alternate fingering for B is 3rd string-4th fret, and this makes it easy to play the D and B together.

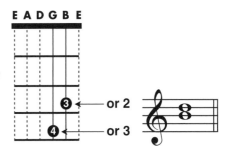

In the following examples, describe how to play both notes. Important hint: always figure out the upper note first!

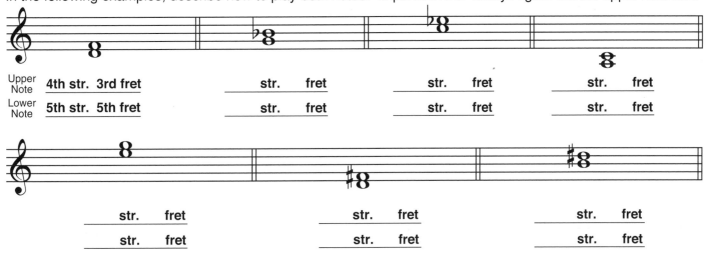

Upper Note	4th str. 3rd fret	str. ___ fret ___	str. ___ fret ___	str. ___ fret ___
Lower Note	5th str. 5th fret	str. ___ fret ___	str. ___ fret ___	str. ___ fret ___

str. ___ fret ___	str. ___ fret ___	str. ___ fret ___
str. ___ fret ___	str. ___ fret ___	str. ___ fret ___

Use after page 16.

The Key of A Minor

Pieces that are written in the key of A minor:

1. have no key signature (no sharps or flats). However, an accidental is often used to raise the 7th tone up a halfstep—in this case, G♯,

2. for the most part, make use of notes from the A minor scale: A, B, C, D, D F, G♯, A,

3. usually end on an A minor chord.

The Three Principal Chords in the Key of A Minor

Minor keys are similar to major keys in that the three principal chords are I, IV and V⁷ chords. However, as you will discover below, in minor keys both the I and IV chords are minor chords; the V⁷ chord is the same as in major keys. With the 3 principal chords in minor keys you can accompany folk and blues songs such as *Joshua Fit the Battle of Jericho*, *St. James Infirmary* and *Hava Nagila*. Minor chords are always written in lower case: i, iv.

The i, iv and V⁷ Chords in the Key of A Minor

Start with the two-octave A minor scale.

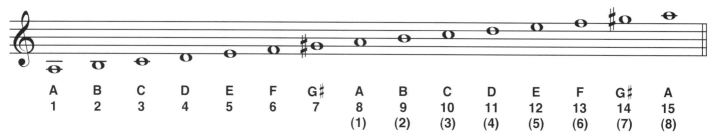

A	B	C	D	E	F	G♯	A	B	C	D	E	F	G♯	A
1	2	3	4	5	6	7	8	9	10	11	12	13	14	15
							(1)	(2)	(3)	(4)	(5)	(6)	(7)	(8)

The i chord starts on the 1st scale tone, A. Using the usual method (see pages 37 and 38), we get A (skip B), C (skip D), E. The i chord in the key of A minor is an A minor chord which consists of the notes A C E.

The iv chord starts on the 4th scale tone, D. Using the usual method, we get D (skip E), F (skip G♯), A. The iv chord in the key of A minor is a D minor chord which consists of the notes D F A.

The V⁷ chord starts on the 5th scale tone, E. Using the usual method, we get E (skip F), G♯ (skip A), B (skip C). D. The V⁷ chord in the key of A minor is an E⁷ chord which consists of the notes E G♯ B D.

i

Am

iv

Dm

V⁷

E⁷

Questions to Answer

What are the three principal chords in the key of A minor?

Name the notes in a D minor chord.

What are the notes in an E⁷ chord?

What are the notes in an A minor chord?

What is the key signature of A minor?

Since both A minor and C major have the same key signature, how can you tell the difference between them? (Hint: think scales and final chords.)

Use after page 18.

$\frac{6}{8}$ Time

The upper number of the time signature means that there are 6 beats in each measure. The lower number means that **each eighth note gets 1 beat**. Practice writing the $\frac{6}{8}$ time signature on the staff to the right:

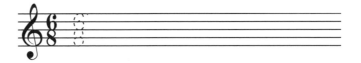

In $\frac{6}{8}$ time, the 6 eighth notes are written in 2 groups of 3. Study the correct and incorrect examples below. (Notice that in the correct examples, the 1st and 4th beats are clearly shown.

Correct

Incorrect

$\frac{6}{8}$ time is commonly heard in folk songs (*Greensleeves, Drink to Me Only with Thine Eyes*), Irish jigs (*Irish Washerwoman, Paddywack*), Christmas carols (*The Wassail Song, Silent Night*) and many other types of music. Many early rock tunes were written in $\frac{12}{8}$ time, which is like two measures of $\frac{6}{8}$ time (Sonny and Cher's *I've Got You, Babe*, for example). However, $\frac{6}{8}$ is hardly ever used in jazz or country music.

Music in $\frac{6}{8}$ time, which is slow to moderately fast, should be played "in six," counting 6 beats to the measure:

Drink to Me Only with Thine Eyes

Sweet Betsy from Pike

When $\frac{6}{8}$ time is played at a faster tempo, it should be counted "in two," that is, 2 beats per measure. Remember that each beat will now contain **three eighth notes** or their equivalent. Here are two examples from familiar tunes.

The Farmer in the Dell

Row, Row, Row Your-Boat

...Mer-ri-ly, mer-ri-ly, mer-ri-ly, mer-ri-ly, life is but a dream.

42

Use after page 24.

The Key of D Major

Pieces that are written in the key of D major:

1. have a key signature of 2 sharps. These sharps are F and C, which means that all F's and C's are played as F♯ and C♯, unless preceded by a natural,

2. for the most part, use notes from the D major scale: D E F♯ G A B C♯ D,

3. usually end on a D major chord.

On the staff below, practice writing the key signature of D major with various time signatures such as $\frac{4}{4}$, $\frac{3}{4}$, ¢, and $\frac{6}{8}$. Remember that the key signature precedes the time signature. When writing the two-sharp key signature, the F♯ always precedes the C♯.

The I, IV and V⁷ Chords in the Key of D Major

Start with the two-octave D major scale.

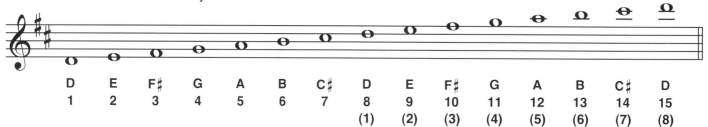

D	E	F♯	G	A	B	C♯	D	E	F♯	G	A	B	C♯	D
1	2	3	4	5	6	7	8	9	10	11	12	13	14	15
							(1)	(2)	(3)	(4)	(5)	(6)	(7)	(8)

The I chord starts on the first scale tone, D. Using the usual method (see pages 37 and 38), we get D (skip E), F♯ (skip G), A. The I chord in the key of D major is a D major chord, which consists of the notes D F♯ A.

The IV chord starts on the 4th scale tone, G. Using the usual method, we get G (skip A), B (skip C♯), D. The IV chord in the key of D major is a G major chord, which consists of the notes G B D.

The V⁷ chord starts on the 5th scale tone, A. Continue as usual with A (skip B), C♯ (skip D), E (skip F♯), G. The V⁷ chord in the key of D major is an A⁷ chord, which consists of the notes A C♯ E G.

Questions to Answer

Name the I, IV and V⁷ chords in the following keys:

KEY	I CHORD	IV CHORD	V⁷ CHORD
C major			
A minor			
G major			
D major			

On the staff below, write the key signatures called for:

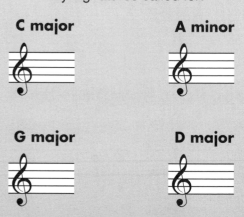

Finding the Root Bass

The **root** of a chord is the note that names the chord. For example, the root of a C major chord is C; the root of a D⁷ chord is D, and so on.

The following chord diagrams show the fingering of every chord you have learned. On each diagram, circle the root of the chord.

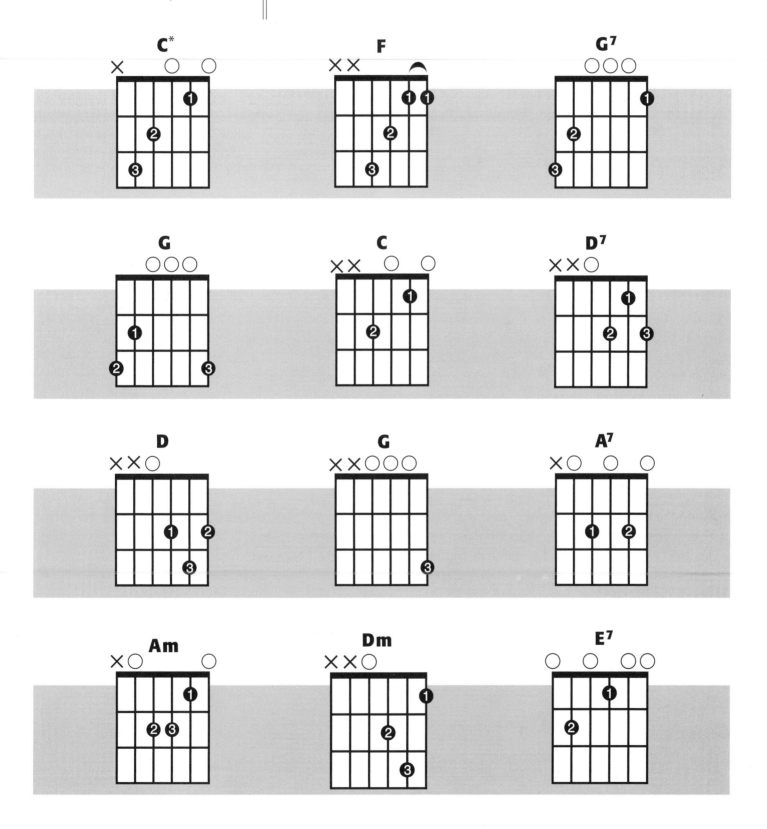

*In cases such as the C chord, which has two C's on the diagram, always circle the lower one.

Use after page 27.

Dotted Notes

A dot just to the right of the head of any note adds half its value to the original note. For example, a half note gets 2 beats; a dotted half note adds half of 2 (1) to the original 2 beats, to make a total of 3 beats. When a quarter note is dotted, it gets 1 beat plus a half of 1 beat (an 8th note), for a total of 1½ beats.

A dotted 8th note gets ½ beat plus a half of a half beat, that is, a total of ¾ of a beat. Think of each beat as containing 4 16th notes. Since an 8th note equals 2 16th notes, a dotted 8th note equals 3 16th notes. Study the next 3 staffs for examples of how to play dotted notes.

Dotted half note = half note + quarter note. Or, think 3 quarter notes tied.

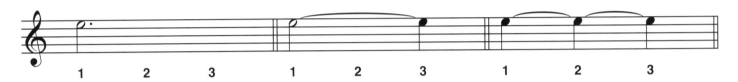

Dotted quarter note = quarter note + 8th note. Or, think 3 8th notes tied.

Dotted 8th note = 8th note + 16th note. Or, think 3 16th notes tied.

In ⁶⁄₈ time the 8th note gets 1 beat. This means that a dotted 8th note gets 1½ beats, just like a dotted quarter in ³⁄₄. Here are 2 examples of well-known melodies in ⁶⁄₈ that make use of the dotted 8th note. Write the numbered beats below the staffs:

Silent Night

Greensleeves

Use after page 30.

Alternating Bass Notes

As you have learned, the root of a chord can substitute for the full chord when creating an accompaniment. A typical pattern in $\frac{4}{4}$ might be Root-chord-chord-chord or Root-chord-Root-chord.

In $\frac{3}{4}$ time, the pattern might be Root-chord-chord.

These patterns can be made more interesting by using Alternate Bass Notes (ABN). In $\frac{4}{4}$, this might be Root-chord-ABN-chord. In $\frac{3}{4}$ time, assuming the chord does not change, the pattern might be Root-chord-chord, ABN-chord-chord.

Alternating bass notes are used to enrich the accompaniment when the harmony remains the same for several consecutive measures.

An alternate bass note can be any low note that is part of the chord, other than the root.

Both the 3rd and the 5th can be used as alternate bass notes, with the 5th more common.

This chart tells you what alternate bass notes are available for each of the chords you have learned.

Chord	Root	3rd	5th	7th*
C Major	C	E	G	
F Major	F	A	C	
G Major	G	B	D	
D Major	D	F♯	A	
A Minor	A	C	E	
D Minor	D	F	A	
G⁷	G	B	D	(F)
D⁷	D	F♯	A	(C)
A⁷	A	C♯	E	(G)
E⁷	E	G♯	B	(D)

Go back to page 43 and, using the diagrams printed there, mark where the alternate bass notes of each chord can be found. You can use "ABN" to indicate the alternate bass notes.

*The seventh is rarely used in the bass.

Use after page 34.

Triplets

Three 8th notes beamed together with the number 3 placed either above or below the group are called an **eighth-note triplet**. This means that 3 8ths are played in the same time as 2 8th notes; in other words, in 1 beat. The 8th-note triplet is common in all types of music, especially early rock 'n' roll doo-wop ballads, where the triplet was used almost exclusively as the accompaniment pattern. Triplets can be counted by saying "one-trip-let" "two-trip-let" etc., making sure, however, that each syllable is equal to every other one.

On the staffs below add a "3" where a triplet is desired. (Ordinarily, the 3 is placed near the beam.) Then complete the count below the staffs:

1   2 trip-let 3   4 trip-let   etc.

Complete the measures below by adding 1 or more 8th-note triplets where appropriate.
Use notes of your own choosing.

A typical doo-wop accompaniment pattern:

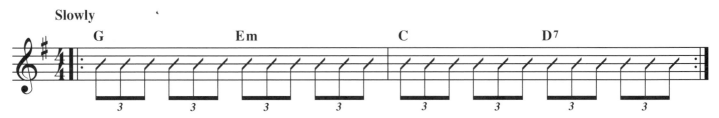

The Key of E Minor

Pieces that are written in the key of E minor:

1. have a key signature of one sharp, the same as its relative key of G major. That sharp is F♯, and this means that every F in the piece is played as F♯, unless preceded by a natural. However, an accidental is often used to raise the 7th tone up a half-step—in this case, D♯,

2. for the most part, make use of notes from the E minor scale: E F♯ G A B C D♯ E,

3. usually end on an E minor chord.

The i, iv and V7 Chords in the Key of E Minor

Start with the two-octave E minor scale.

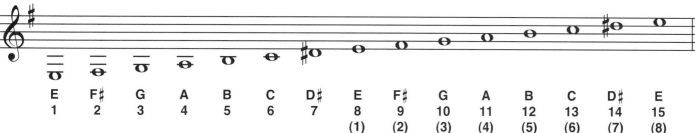

E	F♯	G	A	B	C	D♯	E	F♯	G	A	B	C	D♯	E
1	2	3	4	5	6	7	8	9	10	11	12	13	14	15
							(1)	(2)	(3)	(4)	(5)	(6)	(7)	(8)

The i chord starts on the 1st scale tone, E. Using the usual method (see pages 37 and 38), we get E (skip F♯), G (skip A), B. The i chord in the key of E minor is an E minor chord, which consists of the notes E G B.

The iv chord starts on the 4th scale tone, A. Proceeding as usual we get A (skip B), C (skip D♯), E. The iv chord in the key of E minor is an A minor chord, which consists of the notes A C E.

The V7 chord starts on the 5th scale tone. Proceeding as usual we get B (skip C), D♯ (skip E), F♯ (skip G), A. The V7 chord in the key of E minor is B7, which consists of the notes B D♯ F♯ A.

Questions to Answer

What are the three principal chords in the key of E minor?

Name the notes in an A minor chord.

Name the notes in a B7 chord.

Name the notes in an E minor chord.

Name three ways you can tell if a piece is in the key of E minor:

1. It has a key signature of _____.

2. It gets most of its notes from the _____ scale.

3. It usually ends on an _____ chord.

48

Use after page 38.

The Key of F Major

Pieces that are written in the key of F major:

1. have a key signature of 1 flat, and that flat is B♭. This means that all B's are played as B♭, unless preceded by a natural,

2. for the most part, make use of notes from the F major scale: F G A B♭ C D E F,

3. usually end on an F major chord.

Practice writing the key signature of F major on the staff below. Notice the placement of the flat, directly on the middle line B.

The I, IV and V⁷ Chords in the Key of F Major

Start with the two-octave F major scale.

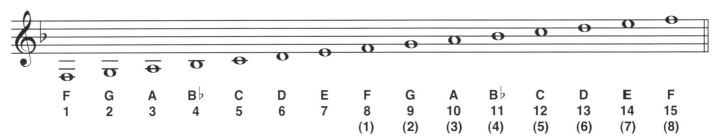

F	G	A	B♭	C	D	E	F	G	A	B♭	C	D	E	F
1	2	3	4	5	6	7	8	9	10	11	12	13	14	15
							(1)	(2)	(3)	(4)	(5)	(6)	(7)	(8)

The I chord starts on the 1st scale tone, F. It contains 2 additional notes, which can be found by going up the scale and skipping a tone between each chord tone. Start with F (skip G), A (skip B♭), C. The I chord in the key of F major is an F major chord, which consists of the notes F A C.

The IV chord starts on the 4th scale tone, B♭. Using the same method as for the I chord, you get B♭ (skip C), D (skip E), F. The IV chord in the key of F major is a B♭ major chord, which consists of the notes B♭ D F.

The V⁷ chord starts on the 5th scale tone, C. Continue as usual: C (skip D), E (skip F), G (skip A), B♭. The V⁷ chord in the key of F major is a C⁷ chord, which consists of the notes C E G B♭.

Questions to Answer

What are the three principal chords in the key of F major?

Name the notes in a B♭ major chord.

What are the notes in a C⁷ chord?

What are the notes in an F major chord?

Name three ways you can tell if a piece is in the key of F major:

1. It has a key signature of _____ .

2. It gets most of its notes from the _____ scale.

3. It usually ends on an _____ chord.

This completes the theory for *Alfred's Basic Guitar Method,* Books 1 and 2. After completing those two books and this one, you will be ready for the exciting world of more advanced guitar playing.